T0137548

AS MY EYES
OPENED

Kisha M Allgood

WESTBOW
PRESS®
A DIVISION OF THOMAS NELSON
& ZONDERVAN

WestBow Press books may be ordered through booksellers or by contacting:

WestBow Press
A Division of Thomas Nelson & Zondervan
1663 Liberty Drive
Bloomington, IN 47403
www.westbowpress.com
844-714-3454

ISBN: 978-1-6642-9206-2 (sc)
ISBN: 978-1-6642-9207-9 (e)

Library of Congress Control Number: 2023902408

Print information available on the last page.

WestBow Press rev. date: 02/09/2023

I

Haunted houses are a cruel joke on a visually impaired person. The floor is uncharted. The walls are foreign. Hands reach out. I feel warmth. I am cold. I feel footsteps, I think I hear someone. A breath on my shoulder. I think I heard my name. Being called into the darkness. I am being watched. By who? Sounds I can't place. From what? From where?

I know what a haunted house feels like. My home used to feel like one. I have very sensitive eyes and ears, and I know that ghosts do not exist. My room is dark. Door shut. Windows Shut. Dark. Darkness in every corner. Shifts and moans I cannot place. I see my mirror in front of me. The shadows around it. I just want peace. I feel like I'm invading space. I just want peace. I just want the light.

Listening is a full body experience. The words moving through my fingers. The comma becomes a breath that leaps from my lungs. Bold. Italic. Line, Period. Line. I am not falling. I am not falling, I can't trust myself. This was a nightmare without a name.

This story is calling me but I can't focus. Undeveloped embryo forces into the world by hands I could not see. I was sleeping in peace only to be disturbed. I was taken from the only shelter I knew. The echoes of a safe space. I was not safe anymore. Removed from my mother. The only home i knew.. I was named Kisha

A recurring image in a rearview mirror. Cars whizzing pass me on Kennedy Boulevard and New Jersey City University a blur. Wheel turning. Noise all around me. Hands on a wheel. Eyes struggling to see.

A white room to the left of the nurse's station. Cries growing longer and louder. My father is standing next to my mother. A soft blanket on new skin. A hand to my hair. I was taken from warmth but a voice I could not forget.

The human eye. Complex sand in an hourglass. I have wide black eyes that shine bright. Diamonds in the deepest mines. Mining for the gold. Warm like hot chocolate. I am liquid warmth. The mahogany crib with a cotton throw covering a body that would not calm down. A wooden chair trimmed in blue and white. Being hummed to sleep. Heat from head to toe. A warm cheek. My mother and I. I feel safe. I am no longer scared.

Years later I sat in the waiting room of an enormous labyrinth. A labyrinth in the city that never slept. A labyrinth in New York City. A labyrinth known as Roosevelt Hospital. The surgery that would change my vision forever. A middle school student facing an exam way beyond her knowledge. Ambulances vibrating through my body. Bleach creeping up my skin. An imaginary wind. Heart. Lungs. I must remember to breathe.

II

I have vertigo.

An invisible illness that can be cured by the remedy I am allergic to. I am allergic to Penicillin. Penicillin injections will eliminate the disorientation and weakness that affect my limbs through every untimed episode. I am on the cusp of delivering. I feel the change but no one can see it. My eyes are not only natural but spiritual. I am an expansive sea of compassion and empathy. I reach out and embrace many. I could walk with my eyes to the ground because of shame, but I walk with my eyes looking forward. I was taken from my mother and placed on a floor that blurred. I was in the Neonatal Intensive Care Unit.

The sixth floor of Mount Sinai Hospital. Light as a feather. Warm and heart beating. I was so tiny, but despite my size I thrived. The world I entered. The world of crying, chatting, and dissipating voices. The reception desk with phones buzzing. The noise rattling the window that peered into the room. The room where I slept. As I walked, the voices got louder, As I walked, darkness wrapped around me. I wasn't walking when I came out, but I found my footing.

I couldn't walk up the stairs. I looked up but could not focus. I was three years old. An undeveloped vision within a developing body. Clarity was elusive to me. Elementary school was a lonely place for a little girl who struggled to see. I couldn't see and there was no one there to see me. Holding the handrail and taking it a step at a time was frustrating. I could not run up the stairs like everyone else. I do not see like everyone else. I tried but I was so uncoordinated.

III

I am an avid reader. I read more than books. I observe. I absorb. I listen. Every spine that passes my fingertips. Arms around the back. I am listening to a story. A story with missing pages. Faded words. Books. Breathing libraries. Language. I can't speak. Feelings. I can't feel. Words I must say.

I don't know why I don't feel like writing. Writing is something I love. I have stories I want to write but I don't know how to write them. I know I should just sit down and write but I just don't know. There is so much in my mind and I can't make sense of it all. The story I want to tell is one that people will look away from. Do I stand accused?

I was being prepped not for an exam I never studied for, but for a surgery that would change my perception of life. I was told to strip and put on a hospital gown. I was then tucked into a bed. I was put to sleep. It was not my bed. Nor my bedroom. I was in the operating room. I was under anesthesia. I was told to lay back and relax. I was nervous. I couldn't relax. With wires in my arm, the room went black. Numb. Disconnected. Without Feeling.

I was diagnosed with vertigo as an eighth grader. A prolonged journey of the unexplainable. There is a continuous prayer in my heart that God with all his love and power will restore my vision. That glasses, dilation, and eye appointments will cease to exist. Whatever his will may be for my vision I am willing to receive it. I will wake up one day and not reach for glasses. I will be able to see and experience the joy and triumph of those around me. I will publish my words. I was formed and filled and will continue to surrender my gift of expression to the One who gave me my voice. I surrender myself to the Lord God Almighty. I no longer have vertigo because I was healed of it. I was healed not by doctors or medicine but by God himself. He removed my vertigo at 27. He removed vertigo after 15 years.

My bedroom with its white walls and cluttered bookshelves. A mirror across from my bed and a closet to my left. A scattered, preoccupied table with four legs that carry the stressful collection of a college experience. The windows are covered by a curtain and endless storage bins keeping the wind from creeping through the thin and aging window panes. Panes carrying the sighs, tears, and fears of people, Pains kept quiet until the house was completely still. The darkness that descends.

IV

As I walk the campus of New Jersey City University, people see a fair -skinned, short haired, five-foot four female with oval glasses and a short peacoat. They don't see the weary glance. They don't feel the pressure. They think they know what they know, but they are blind to the truth.

I have been a full -time college student for the past five years. Five years I don't regret. I graduated from New Jersey City University in 2018 not by my academic knowledge but because I surrendered all the educational confusion to the Lord. I could say I deserve it but NJCU was the training ground of education yet to be accomplished. I am currently enrolled in a Master's program for mental health at Pentecostal Theological Seminary praying and leaning on the Lord.

I was homeless and looking for a place to rest my soul but looking for a home where I would be fed was hard. Being in a completely different state was new for me. I left New York after middle school without knowing anything. I graduated high school and then struggled applying and remaining in college. Narratives of the past echoing in my heart but my mind focused on the words of the Lord. Not knowing is a scary place to be. Being in unknown territory is scary. A new chapter was beginning and God already had it written. I now belong to a beautiful spiritual family. I was chosen to serve not by what I have done but what Jesus did for me. I pray not through selfishness as I once did because I did not understand the gift that was given to me. I pray not to change God's mind or pull his arm, but I seek to just be with Him and grow deeper in Him. Walking alone as the baby Christian I was would lead me to stumble and choose not to walk at all, but God already knew the adoptive family full of his children that I would join. Waiting on Him gave me so much more. I was given a support system of women that I love, care for, and pray for to this very day. I cannot put into words how valuable my relationship to God is to me. Through God I am able to cultivate my love of writing and share it with the world.

V

I hold my breath while my pen bleeds. It bleeds. It cries. It bleeds some more. I was the pen that bleed. I could not write. I couldn't exhale. I could not see. If I was to scream the windows would break. I wanted to throw things. I wanted to run. I didn't throw things. I didn't run. I froze. I screamed once I was cut from my mother's stomach. A scream I have screamed for many years. A scream of the unexplainable. Frustration within me is bubbling, but I hold my tongue. I can't speak of this but it calls. This is my inherited story.

Keeping the lights on, food in the fridge, and

heat in the apartment was tough at times but we managed the best way we could. Feeding a baby on a fixed income is hard, raising a family on a fixed income is hard, but my parents took that on so that I would have a place to stay, food to eat, and clothes on my back. My mother gave up working as a cashier at the local grocery store because I was not sleeping at night. Crying in the dark. Stumbling in the dark. I can't find my way. Living in New York shifted to New Jersey and I have remained where God planted me for the past 17 years

My hands were an engraved map in a sea of darkness. I stumbled helplessly to the bathroom. I had to go. I could not hold it. My bare feet on cold wood and the wind blowing against my fingertips. Grabbing the knob, the checkerboard floor of relief was under my feet. My left hand grabbed the vanity as my right hand searched for the toilet seat. I finally sat down. And then I turn to my left and take two steps in. I grab the vanity and then reach for knobs. The water runs. I turn the water off. I then began my stumbling walk back to bed. Laser Eye Surgery was more than twenty years ago, and throughout the process, the gift of seeing brings me back to the One that formed my eyes in the beginning

VI

I am in the Potter's hands. In the hands of God. Growing and changing daily. From my hips to my waist. Down my legs to my feet. From my wrist to my fingertips. From head to toe. I was formed in my mother's womb. I was crafted by the bodies that laid unashamed in bed. I was their promised seed. I became their daughter. Two Hundred and Eighty Days. Nine months. One day. The beginning of life.

March 6th 2016, the day water called my name. The anticipation of going into a familiar space. I breathe out and let my eyes close. I go gently into the water. A space I thought I would never be but

I was so gently led to I was submerged in a peace that is unexplainable. I felt someone wrap their arms around me.

I was knitted in the womb of my mother. I was born from the womb and entered the world. The Lord gave sight to the blind, hope to the hopeless, health to the sick, and restoration to the poor. I see healing. I am a living soul that is covered by flesh and has all her natural senses. I can hear, I can touch, I can talk, I can taste, I can smell, but I can't see properly.

To some it may look like I am praying into the air with my eyes closed and arms raised, but I am not praying to nothing. I am connecting with and talking to God. My lips may not move and I may seem like I am in a trance state, but I am not. I am talking from my heart. You don't see my heart but when I am in a room I feel the hearts of others. My eyes may be closed but I am conscious of who is around me. I am mentally and physically present in the room, but my spirit opens and my heart expands in prayer.

VII

An eight year old girl sitting on the floor of her room weeping and wondering if healing will ever be. Growing up but remaining teachable before the Lord is receiving the most precious connection. The reconnection to my Father would occur eight years later. At 16 I would say yes and then writing began to make sense. The poet never slumbers in me. The poet is always stirring. My outer vision may be weak, but internally I am being restored. A princess in the clothes of a servant. A thirst for more. A prayer neverending. Me walking in victory.

A conversation with someone could be a prayer.

A prayer of being heard responded with someone listening completely to what you have to say. Slowly entering the room I sit down on the bed. My hands are steady. My voice is soft. My heart is reaching. Eyes that look away from me with a head hung in shame. I kneel down and see hands that are shaking and a lip that is trembling. I gently rest my hands. I may not understand but I do see. I see you.

VIII

The roundness of the door knob, the straight back and rounded shoulders of the windows that long to be opened. Desks prepared to receive students and a teacher yet to enter. Markers resting and waiting to be used. The only color that never dries is green. Green is invisible to me on a whiteboard. It can't be seen.

The leaves of trees and blades of grass fade. The air is colorless. The sun that I love but my eyes cannot adjust to. I love taking walks but I have to walk on the perimeter of what I seek. I seek the sunlight, I am a flower. I close my eyes and observe the song of the birds and the laughter of the children as they aim for the sky. A walk in Lincoln Park. Nature is where I love to be. Listening deeper helps me see deeper.

I hide sometimes. I want to get away sometimes. It can be so bright and loud that I can't adjust. I like my cocoon, but I realize a cocoon is withholding my flight. I understand the need for silence, I understand stillness. Stillness is where I hear the most. I am most present when I don't speak, I become a room.

Walking into that forbidden space makes the walls shake. The heart is indecipherable. The heart is a treasured story. A story I seek. A library I have yet to investigate. I am literature. Vulnerable. Unveiled. Glasses off. A new truth yet to be seen. Like the barcode on the back of a freshly purchased book with its glistening cover, I was a story yet to be read.

The blurriness. My hands. My words. Computer. Mouse. Frustration. Typing and erasing. Page by page. The number on the top of the page glaring at me. Twelve Point Font and struggling. Accepted font but a visual challenge.

IX

I could not hear but something was happening. I have ears but nothing to respond to. I remember that moment. A kiss on my forehead. Warm, safe, motherly. A scent: a scent of home. The scent faded as I was placed in a glass encasement. An encasement that a doll would be placed in at a museum. Four walls of frosted reflections. I was wheeling further and further. That recognition. Mechanical voices with hisses and clicks filled my ears. My ears are slowly opening to the world. The shadows of white coats and crying, that was the beginning of my life.

Babies lined in neat rows. A river of pink and

blue. Color coded identification bracelets. The numbers on my ankle and wrist were the codes that matched a woman in the maternity ward to me. I gave a footprint. Five toes on a cold piece of cardboard. I was here. My signature given.

I was weighed. 5 pounds. 7 ounces. A cold metal slab with a fresh body on it. Squirming and tensing. Stubborn and detached. Hands all over me. Not my mom's. Not my dad's. Just hands. Involuntary movement. My toes wiggle. My nose crinkles. My heart beats. I'm here, I can hear. Warm. Cold. Opposites.

Thick frames, oval shaped. My entrance into the world. Touching texture. Turning pages. Climbing stairs. Looking up and connecting with a loved one. It is easy to believe that looking and seeing are the same thing, but they are not. Looking is momentary and surface but seeing is what scares people.

This labyrinth-like structure located at 1 Gustave L. Leary Place was where I slept scared and alone while my mother was somewhere among the rooms and hallways that went on and on. I cried. I screamed, I tossed. I turned. Shaken. I was born in a hospital. Removed from my shelter. Told that it was time to be born. A chapter in progress. To be continued.

X

A baby responds to their mother's touch. A coo with wide eyes and outstretched arms. Cohen's Fashion Optical, 2877 Kennedy Boulevard. A white coat came in. Appointment. I was told to read what I saw with a camera. Unsteady frame. Broken image. My eyes could not adjust. "Can you read any further" was what the voice floating past my ear was saying. I shook my head, ashamed. I could not read further. Still in the office, cornered. My eyes fought the hand that led a round bottle. The word, unpronounceable. The liquid, threatening. A reoccurrence. It would erase my sight. Dilation drops. A drop in each eye. Eyes getting heavy.

A reoccurring beginning. Chart reading. Note Taking. Dilation. The sun's rays. The invasive rays of the sun stung me. I could hear the voices around me. " Are we going shopping today?" The whizzing of cars clipping the corners of congested intersections. Kennedy Boulevard, a main thoroughfare in New Jersey. I was in Journal Square. Journal Square became louder and louder.

There is a question mark beside visual impairment. The comment reads "No, Kisha is NOT blind or visually impaired". This comment bothers me because they are rejecting the fact that I am wearing glasses because my sight is weak. I needed glasses because I could not climb. "Hello I cannot climb the stairs and no one was there to help me". Crying was my way of saying that I couldn't and no one thought to listen. Kennedy Boulevard becomes 72nd street in Manhattan. My misshapen academic embryo.

I was a flower with a bruised stem. I was a deer in headlights. I was visually impaired. Then came the color green. Green. The color of spring. The color of health. The color of abundance. Yet I stood a beggar. My eyes were combative. My heart was determined. My voice would be heard. Sitting here typing a letter to the vision that has been fighting with me since the day I was born. I can't see. I don't want to see. I can. I will. Yesterday. Today. It's all a blur

XI

Turning on the radio we move the dial to find the right station, just like prayer allows us to tune into God. The space between radio stations are where outer chatter interferes with inner chatter. The thoughts people send out can disturb the messages your heart wants to hear. All I used to hear was static because what I was trying to say was being misinterpreted. Knowing that I need help and asking for it should open up a way for it to come to me, but that did not work at all

"I don't understand". Math was a subject I could not grasp. Sitting in a room on the second floor of Hudson Honors Middle School piecing together problems without solutions. I was in a world where numbers were foreign to me. Lining up my numbers and trying to find the story behind them. There was no story. The numbers held the secrets. I had to bear the glare of eyes that wanted answers I could not find. I raised my hand and looked to my friends for support, I received nothing. Blank stares. I scribbled on my paper trying to locate a door into a world that would never appear. I tried, all I could do was try.

"Kisha hurry up". The impatience around me. The need for something to be done the moment it was assigned. Page. Line. Page. Line. My head hurts. It hurt me. My eyes were tired. My hands were tired. But everyone wanted everything at the same time.

My parents sat in silence. My hands shook as I looked at my parents. They said nothing. Across from my parents sat the faces of women. I don't remember who led the meeting. I don't remember who brought me to the meeting. I was scared, I was worried. I wanted to run. I remember eyes looking at me.

XII

I was a child with an IEP. Individualized Education Plan. Individual meaning me, Education meaning process. Plan meaning aspiration. Physical Therapy. Physical meaning body. Therapy meaning healing. Speech Therapy. Speech meaning voice. Therapy meaning healing. Occupational Therapy. Occupation meaning job. Therapy meaning healing. I was a child. What was happening to me ? I could move but I felt glued to my chair. I could write but I felt suppressed. I could speak but I was ignored.

XIII

Birth order shouldn't dictate much in the family but what do you call a sixteen-year gap? How do you reclaim what time you didn't have? How different is January from November? This is a question still not answered. I let go of being active at school. I was co-editor of a literary magazine and part of the student council. I let go of poetry nights and a talent show. I didn't have social support in high school. Our relationship is just complicated.

A house left dark and dim. The screams within this home come from hearing so much anguish in a low- income community. The screams stemming from being mistreated for thirteen years. The staircase where a five year old girl sat looking at the front door. The disappointment of not hearing a certain key in the lock. I was still sitting on the stairs of my heart waiting for a knock. An apology. Reconciliation. I closed the door of that apartment to start anew in New Jersey. From the area left neglected to a place unknown to me but known to God.

XIV

I feel like I am slowly drifting away from the shore of truth and being pulled into an endless storm of questions. Questions I can't answer. Words not spoken. Lost. Two means a team. Two means a friendship. Two is better than one, as they say. I was born. I existed. I was growing up. I was becoming someone new daily. I was learning. I was in school. I was part of a dance team. I was building a space for me. A space that was missing my sister.. My name is not my own. In one breath my sister named me and with one step she disappeared. I never met the woman I was named after. She mattered to my sister. I never saw her face

Freshman year of high school, Biology. Here we go again. I know that I am a female. I know that I am African American. I know that I am left handed. I wear glasses. I have vertigo. It did not go away. I know I have a name. I was called it by friends and teachers. My name is Kisha.

XV

I know water. Bathwater. I know water. Misty Rain. I know water. I know water. It will always change. I didn't know the truth. All I knew was my name. Words spoken in the darkness. Secrets kept from light. I didn't know. I couldn't see. Amnesia.

I dream of clear vision. I dream of a day that glasses are just a memory. I dream that my eyes will be completely healed. I wish the surgery never happened. I wish was I was never bullied. I wish adults listened to me. I wish that reading didn't cause my eyes pain. I wish that the dark was not so deep. I wish that typing was not the only way. I wish I could just see. I wish that dilation never existed. I wish that I was heard. The world turned its gaze from me. I wish people understood. I wish that patience was a given. I wish friendships weren't so difficult. I dream of a time before my sight changed. I dream of 20/20. I dream of being seen.

XVI

I was cut from my mother's belly. Her belly was my home, My home. My safety. I was not alone. I was conceived. I began to breathe. I am telling my story. I was a promised seed. I came into the world. My mother refused to let go of me. It was a tough pregnancy. My mother fought her diabetes. I was meant to be. I was meant to be seen. I was meant to see. My fight for clarity.

When you lift the heart of someone up in prayer, things start moving and their breath becomes more free. Everything flows from the heart and when the heart is blocked what needs to be done can't even begin. I pray that God lifts any trace of fear, anxiety, uncertainty, sadness, unresolved anger and unresolved pain from your mind,heart, and soul. Your heart is the most important thing to God and I know he will move through it and fix all the broken pieces. He is a healer of broken hearts.

Hope is found in the broken spaces of educational silence and vocal suppression. Hope is found in the broken spaces of creative fear and written truth. I am upon the threshold. I can bravely walk through the door. The disorienting, freefalling, embryo of my life has finally gained its wings. Through faith.

The weight of words that cannot be spoken. The screams that stretched further than me. The tears that have fell longer than mine. The foreign walls of a broken home. The shattered windows. The missing doors. A nightmare is not the house, but the stories that seep out into the night air. A hope of healing. A hope for light. The story. A History. The story of missing stitches. The story of multiple threads. Threads that fray. Threads that bend. God knows the beginning and the end.

The sighs. The tears. The moans. The aches.

The pains. The fears. Ashes rise from the frame. The frame that bears the family. So much weight. Vision, Eyes. Voice. Eyes. Hands. Eyes. My eyes. My breath. My sight.

EPILOGUE

I, Kisha with my hands on this keyboard make an oath to the hands that will lift this story up. Although my hands are sore, my lips parched, and my eyes weak, this narrative is a mirror that I stand bare in front of. Accepting the house that I inhabit although the windows are broken. The curtains that keep the shadows in are gone. The voice that is timid is gone. I, Kisha a work in progress lay bare the most powerful piece of my reconstruction. My magnificent mantra of reclaiming the vision stripped from my being.